MW01245302

Myrita

Becoming a slightly better version of yourself

Louise YT Phua

PARTRIDGE

To order additional copies of this book, contact
Toll Free 800 101 2657 (Singapore)
Toll Free 1 800 81 7340 (Malaysia)
orders.singapore@partridgepublishing.com

www.partridgepublishing.com/singapore

About the Author

Photo by Ng Sok Eng of Berry Happy Photography.

Louise YT Phua is a talent coach for global citizens and international nomads in life and work transitions. Louise thrives in people development. Together with her clients, she constructs work and life plans to help her learners progress.

With over fifteen years' experience in talent acquisition and people development, Louise works with a wide spectrum of talents from various professions, occupations, nationalities, life stages, personalities, motivations, and aspirations.

An avid advocate of lifelong learning, Louise firmly believes that knowledge is everywhere. Whichever profession, hobby, relationship status, or fitness level that one opts for, there is only one barrier to learning—oneself. Learning is an attitude.

A practitioner of appreciative coaching, Louise integrates the concepts of the three dimensions of learning (Illeris 2007), biographicity (Alheit 1999), four modes of recontextualisation (Evans, Guile, and Harris 2011), the theory of possible selves (Markus and Nurius 1986), design thinking (Ideo), ethnography, semiotics, and mindfulness into her practice in learning design and people development. These forward-thinking approaches enable Louise to adopt multiple perspectives and steer her learners to consider roadmaps to overcome obstacles to unleash their talent and achieve their life goals.

A Singaporean by birth, she has worked and lived in Australia, China, France, and Malaysia. While effectively bilingual in English and Chinese, Louise also speaks basic French and Bahasa Indonesia.

Louise holds a Master of Arts in Lifelong Learning from University College London, Institute of Education; and a Bachelor of Arts in marketing and the media from Murdoch University, Western Australia. Louise is a serious practitioner of Mindfulness and Iyengar yoga.

At the heart of it, Louise relishes how each personal story unfolds.

This book is dedicated to Ah-ma, Madame Tay Ah Gek. Ah-ma, you remain one of my most influential and inspirational teachers. It is my blessing to have been a part of your life.

Prologue

Life is a constant flux.

As technologies continue to fuse the physical, digital, and biological worlds, how are you coping with the disruption?

In my practice as a learning designer and talent coach/facilitator of adult learning, I encounter many adults who are ill-prepared for change and disruption. They constantly fumble around trying to determine where they wish to go. When I developed my prototype of a learning toolkit, my learners liked what they saw and quickly adopted it for use.

Hence, *Myrita* was born, inspired by the Spanish name Rita, which means 'pearl'. *Myrita* is a space for you to pause, ponder, and prosper. This journal is a culmination of anecdotes, tools, frameworks, and pearls of wisdom. This booklet aids you as you shift your priorities, or take on new life projects.

Myrita serves a set of prompts and reminders for your lifelong learning journey. As you navigate the disruption in your life, *Myrita* documents your thoughts and deliberate plans for self-exploration, self-awareness, and personal development. *Myrita* is designed for self-directed learners who aspire to become slightly better versions of themselves.

There is no definite magic formula to turn everything into exactly what you want. For that, you need to find the delicate balance between planning to make your goals happen and learning to cope with any disruption that may come along. *Myrita* aims to be your trusted companion in developing and realising your *raison d'être*.

Myrita may be adapted to your coaching practice, educational institution, or learning organisation to cater to specific developmental needs. You may contact me for a coffee chat at *myritabook@gmail.com*.

May we all be well and happy and safe.

Acknowledgements

Several people have made significant contributions to the birth of this publication. I am indebted to the following:

Joseph Wong, a.k.a. Phonetics Joe—you are a great book mentor and grammar Nazi. It was a joy to work with you on my first book.

My parents, grand-parents, brother, sister-in-law, nephews, and entire extended family—in the past, the present and the future. We are always *one* family.

My close friends, training partners, and career supporters—you cast your watchful eyes over my shoulders and help me steer my way around the many obstacles I encounter.

Rain Aronson, yoga teacher and founder of Yoga 109—you set the foundation and paved the way forward for my yoga journey. You taught me the Socratic dialogue that 'no one can teach, if by teaching we mean the transmission of knowledge, in any mechanical fashion, from one person to another. The most that can be done is that one person who is more knowledgeable than another can, by asking a series of questions, stimulate the other to think, and so cause him/her to learn for himself/herself.'

Dr Andrea Creech, previously Reader at UCL Institute of Education— you played a pivotal role in the fruition of my dissertation, 'Portrait of Adult Learners in Higher Education: What Are the Factors That Influence the Capacity to Engage in Deep Learning'. With your close supervision, I learnt to be a meticulous editor of my own writing. You have transformed how I use words to express my thoughts and emotions.

My coaching clients and learners—each time I witness your evolutions, I marvel at your determination to become better versions of yourselves. I salute each and every one of you.

My readers and users of *Myrita*—your active participation and constructive criticism will contribute to even better editions of *Myrita*. I look forward to being of service to you again.

Stay tuned.

With gratitude,
Louise YT Phua

I think therefore I am.

Rene Descartes

I, _____ [name], am
ready to begin a new chapter in my life. I have made a firm decision to
_____ [life project/
new priority].

Me, Right Now

Today

_____ [date]

I am starting my new life by making a difference.

I reside in

_____ [place]

I was born on

_____ [date]

at

_____ [place]

My parents are

_____

_____

My dream is

_____

_____

My strengths are

_____

_____

My next life review is on

_____ [date]

My Guiding Principles

Your guiding principles in life are the values that drive you. Identifying these is important when visualising your dream life. If you are clear about what values matter to you, you will be able to envisage a dream life that incorporates these values. Take a moment to think about what matters to you, and mark the first five values that best define your guiding principles with a star (*).

Acceptance	Drive	Independence	Peace
Accountability	Excellence	Individuality	Perseverance
Action	Family	Integrity	Recognition
Adventure	Friendships	Kindness	Reliability
Authenticity	Frugality	Leadership	Reputation
Balance	Fun	Learning	Security
Beauty	Generosity	Logic	Self-awareness
Candour	Grace	Love	Self-respect
Challenge	Growth	Loyalty	Service
Commitment	Happiness	Leadership	Simplicity
Community	Harmony	Optimism	Sincerity
Compassion	Honesty	Organisation	Spirituality
Courage	Humour	Originality	Strength
Creativity	Humility	Patience	Success
Curiosity	Imagination	Perfection	Wealth

You are never too old
to set another goal or to
dream a new dream.

C.S. Lewis

My Major Goals in the Next
_____ [Weeks/Months/Years]

	What do I want to accomplish?	When will I meet my goals?
1.		
2.		
3.		
4.		
5.		

My Greatest Accomplishment

What are my three major achievements?

_____

_____

_____

From the above, what is my greatest accomplishment to date?

_____

_____

_____

What contributed to my accomplishment?

_____

_____

_____

How can I use this to achieve my current goals?

_____

_____

_____

How can I use this to help myself make future changes to my goals?

_____

_____

_____

What major transitions did I go through in the past two years (e.g. new assignment, new residence, new relationship, etc.)?

_____

_____

_____

How Will I Achieve My Goal(s)?

Where am I now?	How different will I be when I achieve my goal(s)?

*Imagination is more
important than knowledge.*

Albert Einstein

My Allies

Your allies are people who support you in your life goals and purpose. Your allies may be your partners, co-workers, mentors/coaches, family members, friends, or learning buddies. These allies are available and accessible to you at this stage in your life. Identify your allies and engage with them regularly to keep you in your chosen path.

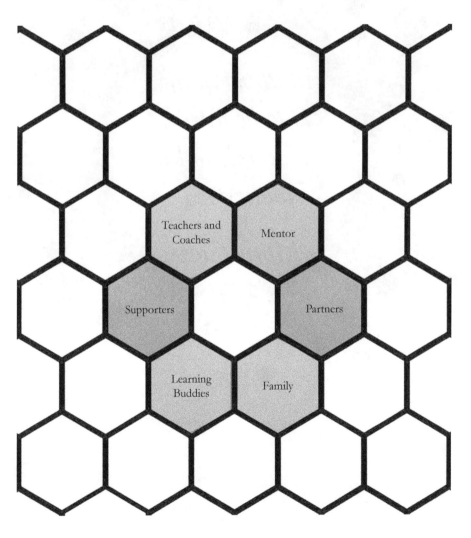

Nothing in life is to be feared, it is only to be understood.

Marie Curie

Key Steps to Achieving My Goals

Step 10

Step 9

Step 8

Step 7

Step 6

Step 5

Step 4

Step 3

Step 2

Step 1

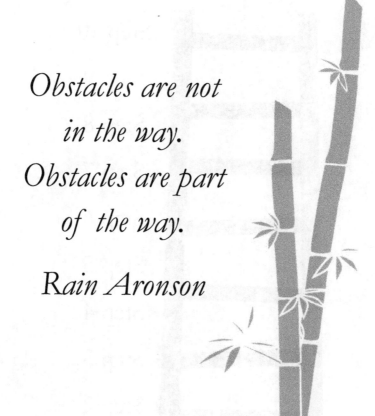

Obstacles are not
in the way.
Obstacles are part
of the way.

Rain Aronson

Additional Sources of Learning

As we now have access to plenty of information, primarily on the Internet and digital space, it is important to identify and discern credible sources of knowledge, and to learn from them.

Good online sources of learning can come from digital magazines, online newspapers, email subscriptions, educational institutions, mentors, industry thought leaders/influencers, books, academic journals, etc.

Thus, creating a structured learning approach provides a disciplined and systematic plan, to build your knowledge and applications to your life project.

Sources	Topics	Frequency of interaction	Rationale

Obstacles to My Development

You will encounter obstacles to achieving your chosen goals. You will be better prepared to face these challenges if you know what they are.

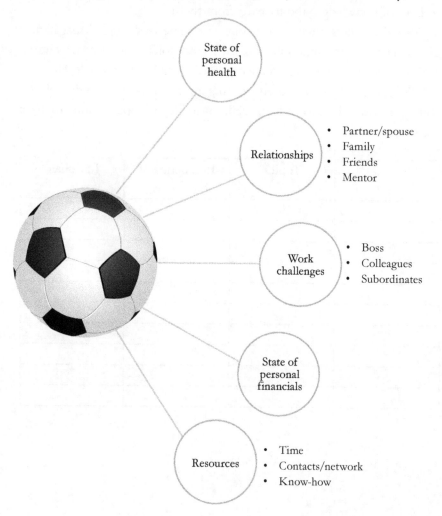

State of personal health

Relationships
- Partner/spouse
- Family
- Friends
- Mentor

Work challenges
- Boss
- Colleagues
- Subordinates

State of personal financials

Resources
- Time
- Contacts/network
- Know-how

According to Plan

Think about this: what tasks are you better at, and which tasks do you struggle with?

Do better at:

_____

_____

_____

_____

_____

_____

Struggle with:

_____

_____

_____

_____

_____

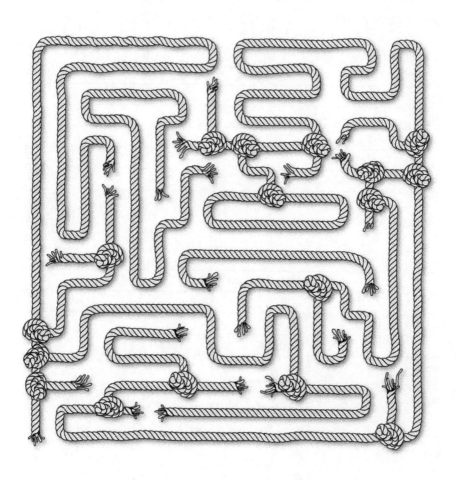

Escape the Grip of Obstacles

Describe the first step for each of the obstacles you have identified.

Obstacles	First steps

I opened two gifts this morning.
They are my eyes.

Anonymous

My Morning Rituals

[1]   Drink a glass of warm water.

[2]   Give thanks/pray.

[3]   Avoid social media for the first hour you are awake.

[4]   Meditate.

[5]   Exercise for thirty minutes.

[6]   Have a cup of tea or coffee.

[7]   Make time for a healthy/wholesome/nutritious breakfast.

[8]   Dress up and smile.

[9]   Declutter your work area.

[10] Learn to prioritise.

[11] Plan your day.

[12] Review your goals.

Sleep . . . Chief
Nourisher in
life's feast.

William Shakespeare

My Evening Habits

[1] Maintain personal hygiene.
[2] Unplug from all electronic devices.
[3] Evaluate your day.
[4] Pen your thoughts.
[5] Plan the next day.
[6] Prepare tomorrow's outfit.
[7] Connect with loved ones.
[8] Practise deep breathing for at least ten minutes.
[9] Read light materials.
[10] Set alarm and put it away.
[11] Dim the lights.
[12] Sleep early.

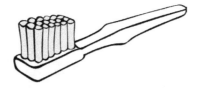

*The journey of a thousand
miles begins with a single step.*

Chinese saying

The Six Best Doctors

The best six doctors anywhere, and no one can deny it,
are sunshine, water, rest, and air, exercise and diet.
These six will gladly you attend, if only you are willing.
Your mind they'll ease.
Your will they'll mend.
And charge you not a shilling.

Wayne Fields in What the River Knows

Are you committing time to the right doctors?

	How often am I interacting with the right doctors currently?	What do I want to do more of?
Fresh air		
Diet		
Exercise		
Sunshine		
Rest		
Water		

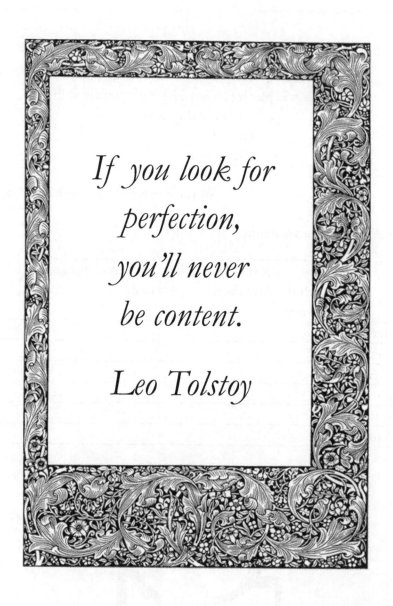

*If you look for
perfection,
you'll never
be content.*

Leo Tolstoy

Things That I Am Thankful For

What are ten things you are grateful for?

1. _____
_____

2. _____
_____

3. _____
_____

4. _____
_____

5. _____
_____

6. _____
_____

7. _____
_____

8. _____
_____

9. _____
_____

10. _____
_____

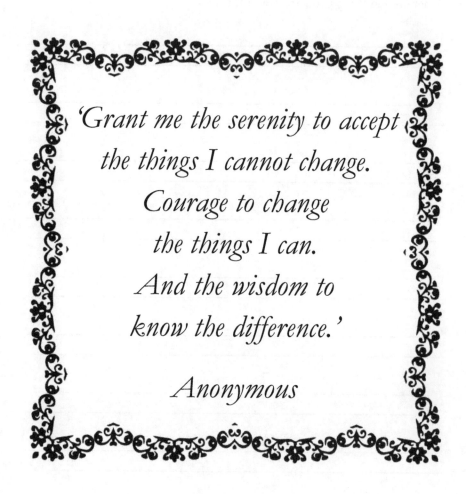

'Grant me the serenity to accept
the things I cannot change.
Courage to change
the things I can.
And the wisdom to
know the difference.'

Anonymous

Distractions Abound

You are distracted every day. These distractions take you away from achieving the goals you have set for yourself. Identify what these distractions are.

All the distractions you have	What can change
	What is out of my control

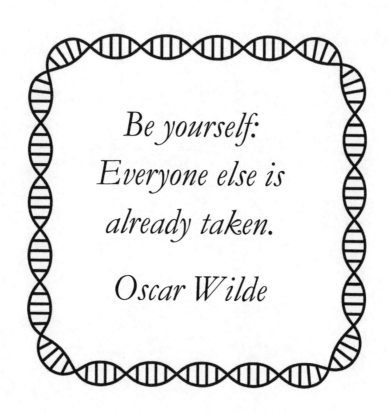

Be yourself:
Everyone else is
already taken.

Oscar Wilde

What Is My Motif?

If you were to create a motif to represent you, what would it look like?
You must be ready to explain your logo.

Feelings come and go like
clouds in a windy sky.
Conscious breathing is my anchor.

Thich Nhat Hanh

Weekly Planner

	Monday	Tuesday	Wednesday	Thursday	Friday	Saturday	Sunday
Morning							
Afternoon							
Evening							
Rewards							

My life is my message.

Mahatma Gandhi

Notes

Notes

Notes

Notes

Notes

Epilogue

Voila! You have practised self-compassion by taking time to pause, ponder, and prospect. Something wonderful happens when you put pen to paper and write down your goals. Every day, you live with purpose when you set your mind to it.

How do you feel after spending quiet time to work towards your life goals?

You are now ready to take concrete steps and real actions towards your life goals. Remember, obstacles are not in the way; obstacles are part of the way.

Stay on course. Stay safe and sane. May you become the slightly better version of yourself that you have set out to become. Let your story unfold.

_____

_____

_____

_____

_____

_____

_____

_____

_____

_____

CPSIA information can be obtained
at www.ICGtesting.com
Printed in the USA
BVHW030959031019
559929BV00020B/33/P